Dolores Found A New Family

True story by:

Corina Rades

and

Dennis Rades

Dolores Found a New Family
Copyright © 2019 by Corina Rades and Dennis Rades

All rights reserved. No part of this publication may be reproduced, distributed, or transmitted in any form or by any means, including photocopying, recording, or other electronic or mechanical methods, without the prior written permission of the author, except in the case of brief quotations embodied in critical reviews and certain other non-commercial uses permitted by copyright law.

Tellwell Talent
www.tellwell.ca

ISBN
978-0-2288-2012-3 (Paperback)

Special thanks and dedication to my family

Chapter 1

Finding a New Home

It was a beautiful summer day, with a warm, gentle breeze rushing through the tree branches and the blades of grass, making the grass look like dancing ocean waves. Dolores had been flying for some time, and she was tired, thirsty, and hungry. Dolores was looking for a safe place to rest. All of the sudden she heard some high-pitched human voices and laughter. She was intrigued and amused by the laughing, so she decided to take a closer look. She perched on a wooden fence that almost camouflage her, as her feathers as well as the fence were both beige. She saw two people, a little boy about five years old and his mother. They were playing in the backyard.

The boy saw the pigeon and shouted. "Look, Mom, a dove."

"That's not a dove, baby," said Mom. "It is a pigeon. A wild pigeon, doves are white."

Then Mom brought some bread and spread breadcrumbs on the fence. And to their surprise, the pigeon walked on the fence very close to them to eat the breadcrumbs. Dolores was very happy to eat the breadcrumbs, as she was very hungry. The little boy and his mother admired the beautiful pigeon. Some of her feathers were beige, and some were like chocolate milk, but there were only few little white feathers sticking out here and there, and her eyes were red.

After she ate, she flew in circles a few times like she was saying, *Thank you for the breadcrumbs...* and then she flew away.

The next day, the pigeon came back. The boy was very happy to see the bird again.

"Mom, the dove is back," he shouted.

"It is a pigeon, baby, not a dove," said Mom. "Doves' feathers are white, but pigeon feathers are different shades of grey, and some other colours, like this beautiful pigeon: beige with white."

Mom brought bread again and spread breadcrumbs on the fence, and the pigeon eagerly ate them. The boy and his mother sat on the grass and watched the pigeon eat. Mom spread breadcrumbs on the grass very close to them, and to their surprise, the pigeon came and ate the crumbs. She was not afraid of the boy and his mother.

"Mom, can we call the pigeon Dolores?" asked the boy.

"Sure, that is a great name for a pigeon," replied the mother.

"Mom, can we keep Dolores? Can we keep her, please?"

"I don't know, baby. She is a wild pigeon. We can't really force her to stay with us. Pigeons are not like a cats or dogs. We can't keep the pigeon in the house or in a cage. She needs a lot of space to fly. She needs to be free."

Dolores took her time eating, and she watched and listened very careful to the boy and his mother. She enjoyed hearing them talking. She walked on the grass, all over the backyard and checked out the two people.

She soared around a little bit, like she was saying, *Thank you for the meal...* and then she flew away.

"I hope Dolores is going to come back tomorrow," said the little boy.

"I hope so too," said Mom.

"I will miss you, Dolores," shouted the little boy.

And what do you know? Dolores came back for the third day in a row. The little boy and his Mom were very happy to see Dolores again. Mom brought bread and spread it right on the grass very close to where the little boy was sitting this time, and then she sat down with him on the grass to see if the pigeon is going to come even closer to them.

And she did.

She was walking in the grass, eating the breadcrumbs and looking at the little boy and his mother. Dolores was enjoying their company. She was not afraid of the people. After she ate, she flew around the people, around the backyard, and all around the house, but she came back and sat on the grass next to the little boy and his mother, this time the pigeon did not flew away.

It was lunchtime, so the little boy and his mother went into the garage to go to the kitchen. When they went inside the garage, Dolores flew right behind them, following them into the garage.

"Mom, Dolores is following us," said the little boy.

"It's okay, baby. Don't be afraid," said Mom. "She's not gone hurt you."

Dolores flew around and checked out the entire garage. It was like she was looking for something very specific, and she liked what she saw because, from that day forward, she never left the little boy and his mother or the house ever again. Dolores let Mom and the little boy pet her. She really enjoyed being petted. Later that day, Dolores met another person, a man. She was not very friendly with the man as he tried to pet her, not like she was with Mom and the little boy. His voice was deeper and more serious than the little boy's and his mother's voice. Dolores pinched him. The man didn't give up though; he talked with her and petted her, and eventually Dolores started to relax around him and allowed him to pet her. And in a short time, Dolores accepted him as a friend and a member of her family. Third time was a charm, Dolores found herself a new home and a family.

Chapter 2

Settling into the New Family and Home

The garage was the perfect place for Dolores. It was close to the backyard, so she could fly in and out anytime she pleased. There was a lot of room in the garage for Dolores to fly and stretch her wings without having to go outside when it was too cold or snowy rainy or windy. Mom made a safe, cozy nest from a wicker basket and hung it in the corner, high above the ground for Dolores to be safe. She made a special place for food and water from an old drawer, and the man mounted in the corner, four feet above the ground where she couldn't be attacked from possible visitors like raccoons, skunks, chipmunks, cats, or mice. Dolores was very happy with her new home and happy to be around people. She would fly and land on their heads and shoulders, and she would gently pick at their hands as a sign of affection. Dolores loved to be around them and listen to them talking, and very often she heard Mom calling the little boy Dennis, and Dennis called the man Dad, so she understood that those were their names.

Chapter 3

Bath Time for Dolores

It was a hot summer, and Dolores need it to have a bath to cool down. But if it wasn't raining, the only water she had was in her drinking bowl. Dennis and Mom watched Dolores struggling to have a bath in that bowl. It wasn't a small bowl, but still it was just a bowl. She would dip her head in first and then her chest, and then she just stepped right in the bowl and sat in it. Dennis and Mom had a good laugh. By the time she was done with her bath there was no water left in the bowl, and her eating and drinking area was a big mess.

"Mom, Dolores needs a birdbath," said Dennis.

"You are so right, honey," Mom said. "We should get her one."

Dad and Dennis went shopping and bought a beautiful birdbath for Dolores. The birdbath was beige the same colour as Dolores' feathers to camouflage her when she bathed. It had three grey bunnies at the bottom of the stand and some green flowers climbing up the stand. They filled it with water and watched Dolores enjoy taking a real bath. Mom was splashing Dolores, and she was splashing everybody back with her wings and her beak. Everybody stood around the birdbath laughing, watching Dolores having fun and getting wet.

Dolores loved the birdbath.

Chapter 4

Losing a Toe

Dolores loved her new home, but there was an unexpected danger in the garage—the chain from the garage door. No one thought of that. One day when Mom and Dennis came home from school, they opened the garage door without knowing that Dolores was sitting on the chain. Once the door started to open, the chain started to move, and it cut Dolores' toe.

Mom took care of the wound, but it was too late, she couldn't save Dolores' toe. So Dolores had three toes on her right foot and four toes on her left foot.

"Mom, do you think Dolores is sad because she lost her toe?" asked Dennis.

"No, baby, I don't think Dolores even knows what just happened with her toe," said Mom. "And she doesn't know how many toes she is supposed to have on each foot or even how to count."

The wound healed nicely, and having only three toes on one foot did not bother Dolores at all. She could walk with no problem. Dad fixed the chain right away. He put a long thin piece of wood along the chain so Dolores could sit on it anytime she wanted without getting hurt. They checked out the garage for any other potential dangers but didn't find any. The garage was the perfect place for Dolores. It was big and safe with a lot of daylight so she could see to fly. It was cool in the summer and warm in the winter. She never got hurt inside the garage again.

Chapter 5

LAYING EGGS

A few weeks after joining her new family, it was time for Dolores to lay eggs. Mom noticed that Dolores didn't fly or go outside for a whole day. She was wondering if Dolores was sick, so she went to pet and talk with her, but Dolores just flew to her eating spot. With the nest empty, Mom wanted to make sure that it was comfortable for Dolores. And when put her hand inside the nest, surprise! There were two little white eggs there. When Dennis came from school and Dad from work, they all cheered for Dolores.

"Oh! Mom, Dolores is gone be a mother."

Dennis was very excited about having baby pigeons.

"You know what, baby? You picked the right name for Dolores because she is female. What If she were male, how would you have named her then?"

"Dolores," said Dennis. "No matter what, she just looked like a Dolores."

Dolores sat on her eggs for about three weeks, but the eggs didn't hatch, so Dolores abandoned the nest. Mom had to make a second nest for Dolores because she wouldn't return to the old one.

So just like that, her family learned that Dolores would lay eggs two month apart, stay on them for about three weeks and then move to the empty nest. Dennis was very disappointed.

"Mom, why doesn't Dolores have baby pigeons?"

"Well, baby," said Mom. "Dolores doesn't have baby pigeons because she doesn't have a mate to be father to her babies."

"Mom, why Dolores doesn't have a husband?" asked Dennis.

Mom pause for a second and then answered her five-year-old boy.

"You see, baby, wild pigeons will mate for life. They only have one husband in their entire life, and if something happens with their mate, they don't want another one, and they will remain single for the rest of their life. There are a lot of other animals out there that mate for life, not only wild pigeons."

Chapter 6

Making a New Friend -- Titi the Cat

One day Dolores' family brought home a little grey and brown kitty. They name the kitty Titi. Dolores was very curious and excited about the little bundle of fur. Little Titi was playful and gentle with Dolores, and in no time, Dolores and the kitty became best buddies. They played and walked together, they took naps together, and they even shared the big red bird house that Dad built for Dolores.

When Mom was gardening, Dolores and Titi would chase each other, ruining all the flowers and vegetables. Dolores would pick the little plants with her beak, and Titi would roll all over everything that was green. But their favourite game was taking turns jumping on Mom's back. It was fun for Mom too, for a while, when Titi was still small, and she hardly felt him on her back. Once Titi grew and become heavy, it wasn't fun anymore because when Titi jumped on Mom's back, it would knock her face down into the flowers. So Mom would shoo them both away, and they would run and fly like two scaredy-cats (well, one scaredy-cat and one scaredy-pigeon).

Other times they would have a third friend to play with because Titi would catch a mouse in the garage and let it go so he could chase it and catch it again so he could let it go… and over and over again with Dolores chasing them both. It was a great show to watch, and no one ever got hurt not even the mouse.

Chapter 7

WALKING THE LITTLE BOY TO THE SCHOOL BUS

It was a joy in the morning for Dolores and Titi was to accompany Dennis and Mom to the school bus stop. Titi would wait by the door, and Dolores would wait outside on the patio's gate for Dennis and Mom to get ready. They would walk behind them on the right side of the street, and Mom would always watch out for traffic. Luckily it was a quiet street. Sometime Titi would run in the grass and hide behind the bushes, and Dolores would fly around a little bit and then come back to walk with Dennis and Mom. It was like circus. Cars and people would stop on the street just to look at Dolores and Titi. Everyone was amazed to see Dolores walking on the street, and not just walking but walking next to people and a cat too.

When they reached the bus stop, all the children would shout, "Look a bird and a cat."

Titi would hide in a nearby bush, and Dolores would perch on the roof of the corner house. They would stay there watching all the kids boarding the school bus. Once the bus left, Mom would walk back to the house, and Dolores and Titi would follow her. Of course, sometimes she would have to chase Titi because he was very easily distracted by anything that moved. But Dolores was always within arm's reach.

Chapter 8

Losing a Member of the Family

As night time came and the family was getting ready to settle for bed, Dad would check to see if Dolores was home, safe in her nest, and Titi was in the house before turning the lights out. One night, Dolores was all set to sleep, but Titi wasn't home. Nobody made a big fuss about it because sometimes Titi spent the nights outdoor, and then in morning he would be waiting at the door to be let inside and fed.

This time morning came, but Titi was not waiting at the door. Mom, Dennis, and even Dolores went to look for Titi all over the neighbourhood. They put up posters with a picture of the missing cat and their telephone number, hoping that someone would call or bring him home. The whole family looked and waited for weeks for Titi to come back home, but it didn't happen. Dennis and Mom were very sad and cried every day because they missed Titi. Even Dolores looked and waited for her old buddy. No one knew what happened to Titi—he just vanished. Mom couldn't stand to see Dennis so sad, so she promised Dennis that they would get another kitty.

Chapter 9

Dolores Loves Human Companionship

Everywhere Dennis and Mom went, Dolores wanted to go too. Sometimes she was allowed to follow them like on short walks around the neighbourhood, but sometimes when they were going to the park, or riding their bicycles, Dolores was not allowed to follow them, and she would stay put on top of the gate, waiting for them to come back home.

The one thing Dolores loved the most was to be around people. She loved Dennis and Dad, but her favourite person was Mom. In between times when Dolores was waiting to lay eggs, she was all over Mom. She would land on Mom's head and shoulders or just cuddle next to her wherever she was sitting. In the morning, Dolores would wait on the windowsill at Mom's bedroom for Mom to wake up, and as Mom moved from bedroom to bedroom to open the windows, Dolores would fly to each bedroom and cling to the window screen just to be with Mom. If Mom had let her, Dolores would have slept in Mom's bed. When the neighbours were outside, she would perch on the corner of their house to hear them talking. Unfortunately, Dolores didn't know that not all people were friendly. But soon enough she learned.

Chapter 10

Dolores Goes to Jail

One day when Mom came home from work, she didn't see Dolores. She called and looked around for her, but Dolores didn't come, and that was unusually because, usually, once she heard Mom's voice, she would come right the away. Mom knew right away that something was not right.

Just then, one of the neighbours who knew Dolores came over and told Mom that Dolores had been taken away by Animal Control. You see, Dolores was free to fly around at any time, even if she was home alone. She'd heard voices in one of the neighbours' garage, and because she loved being around people, she flew right in. Unfortunately, she was not welcome there. The neighbour called the Animal Control, and they took Dolores away. Later that evening, Dennis, Mom, and Dad went to rescue Dolores from Animal Control. Luckily, they found Dolores easily as she was the only wild pigeon there. They put Dolores in a cat cage and drove her home. Dolores was very quiet all the way home, like she was feeling guilty because she'd done something that she was not supposed to do.

After one day in jail, Dolores was very happy to see her family and to be home. She flew onto everybody shoulders and gently picked at their hands. Dolores never flew to that neighbour's garage or house again. She learned her lesson. Never get too close to strangers.

Chapter 11

WELCOME A NEW MEMBER IN THE FAMILY -- TICA THE CAT

One day when her family came home, Dolores was waiting by the door on the front steps, and once they opened the door, Dolores snuck inside between their feet like she often did. She just loved to be inside the house. But surprise, surprise! Mom bent down and put a kitty on the carpet. It was grey and white, and so, so small—it was half the size of Dolores. Dolores was surprised and exited.

The whole family was very excited to have the new kitty at home.

After Titi disappeared, Mom had promised Dennis a new kitty, and so Dennis and Mom went to the Animal Shelter and adopted the smallest and the most playful kitty there was. They named the little fur ball Tica.

She was a little bundle of joy that wouldn't stay still not even for one second. Tica made Dolores tired because she was hunting, chasing, and trying to catch her, so Dolores had to fly every time without rest. Luckily Dolores had more experience with cats than the

Tica had with birds, and she would just sit somewhere higher than the kitty could jump. Let be honest, Dolores was not young anymore, not like when she first met her old buddy Titi. In a short time, Dolores and Tica became good friends. They played and cuddled together and looked out for each other. Dennis and Dolores were very happy to have Tica as their friend.

Chapter 12

DOLORES GETS SICK

On Christmas week, Mom noticed that Dolores was not flying, not eating, and not playing with Tica at all. All Dolores did was walk on the floor and face the corner like she was being punished. She took Dolores in her hands and noticed that Dolores was weak and very hot and that her breathing was very loud.

"That doesn't sound right," Mom said. "You have a cold, poor little thing."

Mom took Dolores inside the house and made a warm nest right next to the heat vent and covered her with a little red blanket so she would stay warm and hopefully sleep to recover. Sleep is the best medicine. Tica tried couple of time to play with Dolores, but Dolores didn't respond to her calls, and Tica understood that Dolores was not feeling well.

Tica sat by Dolores' side every day and night, helping her to get better. She would drink water from Dolores' bowl so Dolores would drink too, she encouraged Dolores to eat and walk by rubbing her nose into Dolores' body, and Tica did that till the day Dolores recovered.

Every day, Mom and Dennis would feed Dolores by hand and give her warm fresh water.

"Is Dolores going to be okay?" asked Dennis.

"Of course, baby," Mom said. "She eats, and she breathes properly, and that is a good sign of recovery."

By the New Year, Dolores was healthy again, with no fever and no hard breathing. She even started to fly all over the house, chasing the cat. That was a very good sign of recovery, except that she needed it to go back in the garage because she was making a big mess everywhere.

But she didn't want to go back and stay in the garage.

She wanted to stay inside the house where she could hear and see everyone. Every time the door was open, she would sneak between people's legs and quietly go to the heater vent even though the basket was not there anymore. It took couple of weeks of hard work for Dolores to understand that she needed to go back to her old nest in the garage. Eventually she did, and she soon forgot all about being sick.

Chapter 13

Pigeons Are Smart Birds

Whenever Dolores needed something, she would find a way to let Mom know. If she was thirsty and didn't have water in her drinking bowl, she would go to Mom and dip her beak in Mom's cup just to let her know that she was thirsty. When Dennis and Dad wanted to play or pet her and she wasn't in a loving, playing mood—or if she wanted to protect her eggs—she would pinch their hand and slap them with her wing. It looked like she was giving a *high five* as the boys had their palm open. Every time someone that Dolores didn't know walked close to the house, Dolores would alert Mom by making an unusual sound that almost sounded like a dog bark. She never *barked* at people that she knew. She just looked out for her family in any way she could.

Chapter 14

DOLORES GET ATTACK BY A HAWK

It was a beautiful spring day, and Dolores was flying back and forth in the backyard to the kitchen windowsill where she could hear and see Mom washing the dishes. She landed on the windowsill, making all kind of noises, like she was talking with Mom who was happily talking back.

All of the sudden, Dolores felt a tight, sharp grip on her body, and was pulled back and up at the same time.

Dolores was being attacked by a hawk!

Surprised and confused, Dolores tried to fly out of the grip. She opened her wings and forced the hawk to let her go. Dolores flew toward garage and, luckily, fell behind the barbecue where she was safe for a few seconds. Then the hawk attacked again.

Dolores was cornered, with no place to run or to fly. It didn't take long for the hawk to put his vicious talons on Dolores again. The hawk was just trying to get a better grip on Dolores so he could fly away with her in his talons. Luckily, at exactly that moment, Mom came outside calling Dolores' name.

When all that struggling happened, Mom heard an unusual bone chilling screeching noise—it was a hawk's foul screeching, followed by a bang.

"What is that?" Mom had asked. "Dolores, are you okay?"

But she couldn't hear Dolores. It was just quiet. She looked outside the window and she couldn't see Dolores on the windowsill. And that was not good. Mom got an empty feeling in her stomach and ran outside.

At the garage door, the hawk was in top of Dolores ready to take off. At Mom's appearance, the hawk let go of Dolores and flew away. Mom took Dolores in her hands and checked her for wounds. Dolores was bleeding from one leg, but just a little bit. It was just a scratch, nothing serious.

Mom didn't know if the hawk had bitten or scratched Dolores or whether she had just been hurt when she fell behind the barbecue. Dolores didn't feel any pain, but she was very scared and was shaking. She was relieved when Mom took her in her hands. Feeling safe, she made herself very small and curled up against Mom's chest.

Mom cleaned the wound and put the basket back in the house so she could keep a close eye on Dolores' wounded leg. Although the wound was very little, Dolores was limping. With good care and a lot of love from all her family members, Dolores recovered in a very short time.

The good thing was that Dolores didn't lose her leg, and the limping went away. Dad mounted a big, black, mean-looking Owl as a decoy on top of the pergola so no hawk would dare to come so close to the house again. Living inside the house was a real treat for Dolores, and she enjoyed it very much, but this time, once she got better, she really wanted to go outside. Dolores went back to the garage and everything went back to normal.

She was flying, walking, playing with Tica, and laying eggs like nothing had happened. She was happy. Dolores was the happiest and luckiest pigeon in the world. She'd found a family that she loved and who loved her right back.

Dolores and her family are very fortunate to have found each other.

www.ingramcontent.com/pod-product-compliance
Lightning Source LLC
LaVergne TN
LVHW051226070526
838200LV00057B/4632